Starting

By Chris Butterworth

CELEBRATION PRESS
Pearson Learning Group

The following people from **Pearson Learning Group**
have contributed to the development of this product:

Joan Mazzeo, Dorothea Fox **Design** | **Editorial** Leslie Feierstone-Barna, Cindy Kane
Christine Fleming **Marketing** | **Publishing Operations** Jennifer Van Der Heide
Production Laura Benford-Sullivan
Content Area Consultant Dr. Daniel J. Gelo

The following people from **DK** have
contributed to the development of this product:

Art Director Rachael Foster
Martin Wilson **Managing Art Editor** | **Managing Editor** Marie Greenwood
Wilfrid Wood **Design** | **Editorial** Julie Ferris
Brenda Clynch **Picture Research** | **Production** Gordana Simakovic
Richard Czapnik, Andy Smith **Cover Design** | **DTP** David McDonald
Consultants Philip Wilkinson

Dorling Kindersley would like to thank: Peter Visscher for original artwork. Rose Horridge, Gemma Woodward, and Hayley Smith
in the DK Picture Library. Johnny Pau for additional cover design work.

Picture Credits: AKG London: John Hios 20bl; Schutze/Rodemann 20t. DK Images: American Museum of Natural History 36b, 37tr;
British Museum 3tc, 3cr, 3bl, 3bc, 4tr, 4bl, 4br, 5bl, 5bc, 5br, 6cr, 7bl, 7br, 9bl, 10tl, 10cla, 10cr, 10clb, 11br, 13cr, 14tr, 19b, 21tr, 21bl,
24tc, 24cr, 24bl, 25cr, 26; Cairo Museum 1; Edinburgh University 16b; National Museums and Galleries of Wales 27tl; Pitt Rivers Museum 35br;
Wallace Collection 28. Getty Images: Penny Tweedie 32b. ImageState/Pictor: 30b. Masterfile UK: Courtney Milne 34b. Rex Features: Sharok
Hatami 17tr. World Pictures: 31t. Jacket: DK Images: British Museum front bl; Pitt Rivers Museum back. Masterfile UK: Dana Horsey front tl.

All other images: ˙ Dorling Kindersley © 2005. For further information see www.dkimages.com

ISBN: 0-7652-5271-6

Color reproduction by Colourscan, Singapore
Printed in the United States of America
4 5 6 7 8 9 10   08

1-800-321-3106
www.pearsonlearning.com

Contents

The Origins of the Modern World

Who developed the first alphabet? Why do people live in communities? What are the origins, or beginnings, of civilization in the world? This book explores these questions. It tells how ancient peoples lived in different parts of the world. It shows how the cultures of ancient peoples—their ideas, arts, skills, and ways of life—have shaped the world we know today and served as starting points for today's civilizations.

This elaborately carved boundary stone is from ancient Babylon.

Early Civilizations

This timeline shows the major civilizations covered in this book. The letter *c* before a date means circa, or about, and means that the date is not exact.

150,000 B.C.	20,000 B.C.	10,000 B.C.	3500 B.C.	2500 B.C.	2000 B.C.	150

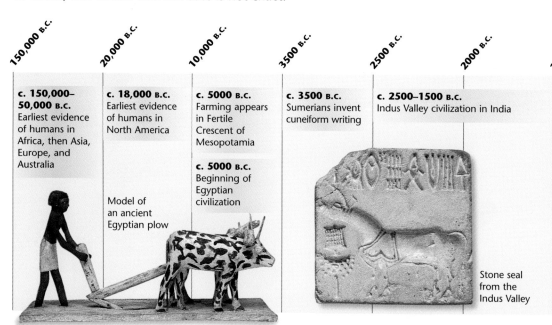

c. 150,000–50,000 B.C.
Earliest evidence of humans in Africa, then Asia, Europe, and Australia

c. 18,000 B.C.
Earliest evidence of humans in North America

c. 5000 B.C.
Farming appears in Fertile Crescent of Mesopotamia

c. 5000 B.C.
Beginning of Egyptian civilization

c. 3500 B.C.
Sumerians invent cuneiform writing

c. 2500–1500 B.C.
Indus Valley civilization in India

Model of an ancient Egyptian plow

Stone seal from the Indus Valley

Scientists believe that many early civilizations began near rivers. People caught fish and hunted birds and larger land animals that came to drink from the river. People used the rivers to water crops and dispose of wastes. People used rivers for travel as well. Boats were one of the earliest forms of transportation.

Civilizations began in different places at different times. There was no simple progression from one time and place to another. Sometimes civilizations made the same discoveries at the same time. For example, both the ancient Egyptians and ancient Polynesians studied the skies to find their way, yet these early peoples lived thousands of miles apart.

How Do We Know About the Past?

Archaeologists study ancient peoples. They dig up long-buried ancient objects, such as buildings, tombs, tools, and pottery, and search for clues about how and when the makers of those objects lived. Archaeologists today often use sophisticated tools and data analysis. They also use computer models, chemistry, and modern atomic theory to help date and interpret objects.

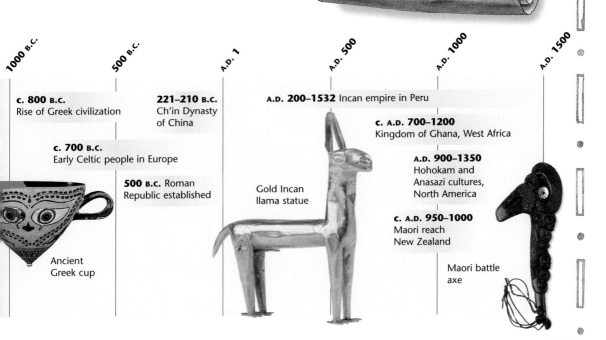

1000 B.C. 500 B.C. A.D. 1 A.D. 500 A.D. 1000 A.D. 1500

c. 800 B.C.
Rise of Greek civilization

221–210 B.C.
Ch'in Dynasty of China

A.D. 200–1532 Incan empire in Peru

c. A.D. 700–1200
Kingdom of Ghana, West Africa

c. 700 B.C.
Early Celtic people in Europe

A.D. 900–1350
Hohokam and Anasazi cultures, North America

500 B.C. Roman Republic established

Gold Incan llama statue

c. A.D. 950–1000
Maori reach New Zealand

Ancient Greek cup

Maori battle axe

Sumerians

The great civilizations of Mesopotamia were found near the banks of the Tigris and Euphrates rivers.

Assyria

Babylon

Akkad

Tigris R.

Euphrates R.

Sumer

Ur

Persian Gulf

One of the first civilizations was in a region called the Fertile Crescent. Here, between two rivers, the Tigris and the Euphrates, people built towns and cities. Beginning around 5000 B.C., the Fertile Crescent was home to several civilizations. This area was also called Mesopotamia, which means "land between the rivers." It is now the site of modern Iraq and eastern Syria.

With plenty of water and a hot climate, wheat, dates, and other fruits and vegetables grew abundantly. By 3500 B.C., a group of people called the Sumerians had settled in this region. Their first small villages soon grew into large, crowded cities. One such place was Ur, where many craftspeople and merchants lived and worked.

Sumerian cart

The Sumerians' greatest invention may have been writing. By 3500 B.C., they began to keep records on clay tablets of what livestock and goods they had. The person who wrote the information is known today as a scribe. The scribe used a sharpened reed, which was pressed into damp clay to make marks. The clay tablet was then dried in the sun.

The earliest writing was picture writing. Pictographs were picture symbols that stood for objects and numbers. Over time, pictographs developed into a script called cuneiform (which means "wedge-shaped," after the triangular marks made in the clay tablets by the reed's sharp tip).

The wheel was probably first invented in Mesopotamia between 5000 and 3500 B.C. However, the Sumerians may have been the first to used the wheel for making pottery. Later, they made carts used to carry goods, and chariots, which were two-wheeled, horse-drawn vehicles.

Buried Riches

Archaeologists have discovered a great deal about the Sumerians by digging into, or excavating, their burial sites. For example, beautifully made gold jewelry and decorations were found in the tombs of kings and queens of Ur. These objects show both the wealth and skill of the Sumerians.

This cuneiform tablet was written in about 2100 B.C.

wedge-shaped marks

Gold headdress, 3000–2500 B.C., found in a royal burial site at Ur

Ancient Egyptians

Thousands of years ago people settled in the valley of the Nile River in northern Africa. They hunted and trapped fish, ducks, and other game that lived in or along the river. About 5000 B.C., they began to farm. Although the area was mostly desert, crops grew well in the Nile Valley. The Nile flooded the valley every summer. The fertile soil left behind when the floodwaters receded was perfect for growing fruits and grains such as figs, wheat, and flax.

The ancient Egyptians learned to store floodwater in ditches, basins, and canals. They used the saved water to irrigate their crops. Not only was the river essential for farming, it was also used for transporting people and products from place to place. Small reed boats and large wooden barges took Egyptians and their products up and down the Nile.

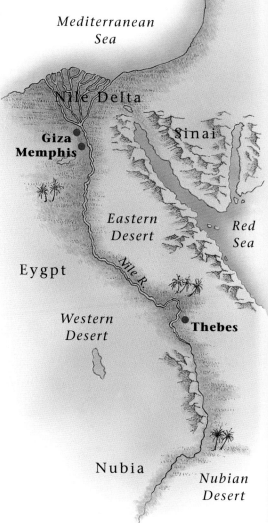

The Nile River was used to transport people and goods throughout Egypt.

This ancient model shows how oxen pulled a lightweight plow through the fertile soil near the Nile River.

Like the Sumerians, the ancient Egyptians invented a system of picture writing, called hieroglyphs. Beginning around 3300 B.C., Egyptians used hieroglyphs for sacred texts and tomb carvings and a simplified form called hieractic to keep records of crops and taxes. Scribes wrote on a paperlike material made from a plant, the papyrus reed.

the statue known as the Sphinx and a pyramid at Giza

hieroglyphs found in the pyramids at Giza

Perhaps the most amazing achievement of the ancient Egyptians was building the pyramids at Giza. These structures were built as tombs for the pharaohs, or kings, of ancient Egypt. The pyramids are still among the largest structures on Earth. What is so astonishing is that the ancient Egyptians built them without modern equipment. Even today, archaeologists are still unsure of exactly how the pyramids were built. Many think that a system of pulleys and levers, as well as thousands of workers, made it possible to place the giant stones.

Hippopotamuses were hunted in the Nile Valley.

Protective charms such as this Eye of Horus were placed in coffins.

Egyptian ring

The beetle symbolized the sun god, Re.

The rule of the pharaohs lasted for about 3,000 years. Pharaohs built palaces and temples. Traders sailed across the Mediterranean Sea. They carried food, cloth, papyrus, and manufactured goods, such as pottery and furniture. Egyptians also brought in, or imported, silver, copper, tin, horses, timber, and wine from other peoples.

At first, Egypt had only a small army of foot soldiers as border guards. Later, Egyptians learned how to build horse-drawn chariots. As Egypt expanded, it developed a large army of well-organized professional archers, swordsmen, and charioteers.

Lasting Legacy

Among Egyptian ideas that influence life today are:
- a solar calendar of 365 days
- a seven-day week
- antiseptics to combat infection
- the idea of the body's circulatory system

Egyptian short sword

Ancient Egyptians believed in life after death, so they buried the dead with food and other items they believed would be needed on the journey to the next world. When a pharaoh or other important person died, the body was mummified, or preserved, for the afterlife.

Mummification took about seventy days. First, the body was washed in salt water. Then the organs were removed and replaced with sawdust. After that, the body was rubbed with oils and covered with salt. When the salt dried, the body was wrapped in linen bandages and adorned with amulets, or good-luck charms. Finally, a mask was placed on the face and the body enclosed in a coffin.

In many ways, ancient Egypt was the model for later civilizations. Egyptian ideas of social order, irrigation and navigation techniques, international trade, a writing system, and beautiful artwork all influenced later thought and technology.

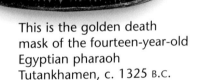

This is the golden death mask of the fourteen-year-old Egyptian pharaoh Tutankhamen, c. 1325 B.C.

This bread was found in an ancient Egyptian tomb and is about 3,000 years old.

Indus Valley Civilization

The Indus River flows through modern-day India and Pakistan. From about 2500 B.C. to about 1500 B.C., the Indus Valley was one of the largest ancient civilizations. The Indus people were the first to grow cotton for cloth. They also kept wheat harvests in large storehouses. On the coasts, merchants sold ivory, cotton cloth, gems, and spices in exchange for tin and semiprecious stones.

Harappa

Indus Valley

Indus R.

Mohenjo-Daro

Arabian Sea

pottery statue of the Indus mother goddess

Mohenjo-Daro and Harappa were the largest cities in the Indus Valley at this time. About 40,000 people lived there in mud brick houses built around courtyards. Each house had its own well and toilets connected to underground drains. Such a sophisticated drainage system did not appear again until the Roman period, which began about 750 B.C.

the Indus city of Mohenjo-Daro

Through their excavations, archaeologists have been able to tell much about the Indus Valley civilization, but many mysteries still remain. They have found numerous small statues of Indus gods, but no great temples. Archaeologists believe the Indus people most likely worshiped in their own homes or at small public shrines. Some areas specially designed for these small statues have been discovered at Indus Valley excavation sites.

The biggest mystery, though, is why the Indus Valley civilization ended around 1500 B.C. Was there a deadly flood on the Indus River? Did drought cause famine? Did invaders drive the people away? Perhaps there was more than one cause. No one is really sure. Archaeologists hope to uncover the answers to these questions in the future.

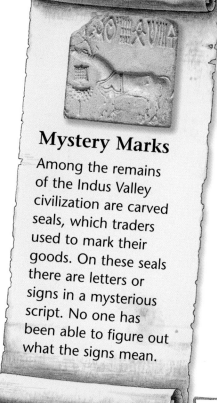

Mystery Marks

Among the remains of the Indus Valley civilization are carved seals, which traders used to mark their goods. On these seals there are letters or signs in a mysterious script. No one has been able to figure out what the signs mean.

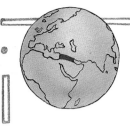

Eastern Mediterranean Civilizations

From the beginnings of Middle Eastern civilization in what is now Iraq and Syria to areas along the eastern Mediterranean, many cultures rose and fell. The civilizations of Canaan, Assyria, and Babylon, important in their own time, are still significant today. Many current traditions can be traced back to them.

Canaan is the ancient name for the land west of the Jordan River, now covered by parts of Israel, Lebanon, Syria, and Jordan. Crops did well in the fertile Jordan and Orontes river valleys. Walled cities such as Gaza and Jericho arose, and their rulers built palaces and fortresses. After 1700 B.C., the Canaanites invented an alphabet with 27 letters. This alphabet is the basis of our modern alphabet.

A skilled Canaanite goldsmith made this pendant in c. 1500 B.C.

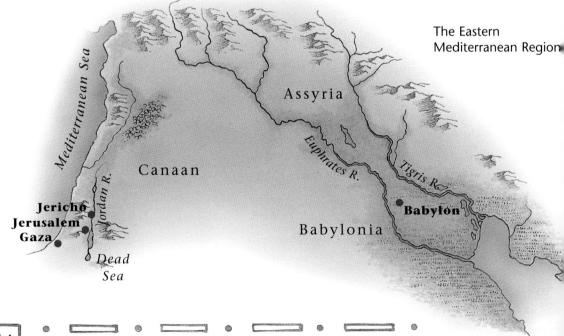

The Eastern Mediterranean Region

Canaan's location as a trade link between the wealthy regions of Africa and Asia made it a tempting target. Through the centuries, many peoples, such as the Semites, Philistines, and Hittites, fought for this land. Egypt controlled the area for four hundred years, from about 1550 B.C. to 1150 B.C.

From their location in what is now Iraq and Syria, the Assyrians moved south to become the most powerful people in the region between 900 and 700 B.C. They defeated the northern kingdom of Israel in 722 B.C. and resettled thousands of Israelites in other parts of the Assyrian empire. A civilization built on conquest, Assyria took its wealth from defeated states, such as Judah. Stone carvings show Assyrian archers driving their enemies across the Euphrates through a rain of arrows.

The city of Babylon, on the Euphrates River, was one of the glories of the ancient world. Around 1800 B.C., its king, Hammurabi, conquered all of Mesopotamia and wrote the Code of Hammurabi. About a thousand years later, an even greater Babylonian empire rose under King Nebuchadnezzar. Using their great knowledge of mathematics, including geometry, the Babylonians designed ornate palaces, gardens, and gates.

Early Laws

The Code of Hammurabi, from about 1800 B.C., is the oldest known set of laws. The code protected all classes, so "that the strong may not oppress the weak, that justice be dealt the orphan and the widow."

The spectacular roof gardens at the royal palace in Babylon were known as "The Hanging Gardens." They were one of the seven wonders of the ancient world. We don't really know what they looked like. This is one artist's idea.

Arabia

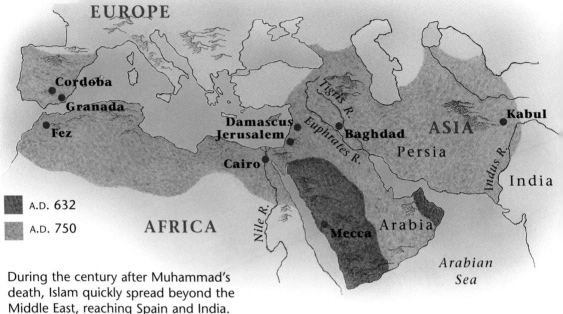

EUROPE

Cordoba

Granada

Fez

Damascus
Jerusalem

Cairo

Tigris R.

Euphrates R.

Baghdad

ASIA

Persia

Kabul

Indus R.

India

A.D. 632
A.D. 750

AFRICA

Nile R.

Mecca

Arabia

Arabian
Sea

During the century after Muhammad's
death, Islam quickly spread beyond the
Middle East, reaching Spain and India.

   The Bedouin people (their name means "desert-dweller"),
who lived in Arabia's northern deserts, were nomads. They
lived in goat-hair tents and moved from one watering place
to another. Their animals fed on the desert plants that grew
after each rainfall.

By 1100 B.C., they
were using camels for
long desert journeys
because a camel can
travel great distances
without water. Camel
caravans crossed the
desert to reach the
busy trading cities of
the West and South.

The Bedouin used camels to carry their belongings
across the vast deserts of northern Arabia.

In the fourth century B.C., the Nabataeans, a northern Arab tribe in what is now Jordan, had the region's most reliable water source. This meant that the Nabataeans controlled the international trade routes that linked China, India, and southern Arabia with Greece, Rome, and Egypt. They traded spices for products such as textiles, grains, and pottery.

Muslim pilgrims in Mecca

One of the world's major religions, Islam, was first revealed to the Prophet Muhammad around A.D. 610. Muhammad was born in about 570 in the city of Mecca. As a young man, he helped drive camel caravans across the desert. He spent much time alone, meditating about faith in God. Early Arabs worshiped many gods, but after years of prayer, Muhammad felt that he had received a revelation from the one God, Allah. When he died in 632, most of Arabia had accepted the new religion of Islam, which means "obedience to the will of God."

Muhammad's new faith spread rapidly west to North Africa and Spain and east to India. Unlike dry, barren northern Arabia, the southern and western coasts of the Arabian Peninsula were fertile. People settled in coastal cities that traded with cities in the Mediterranean, East Africa, India, and China. Islam was also spread through the conquering of peoples, such as the Persians. Arabs ruled Persia for almost 1,000 years, from 651 to 1502.

Islamic Faith

Today, Islam is the second most-practiced religion in the world, after Christianity. Indonesia, Pakistan, India, and Bangladesh have the largest Muslim populations. Followers of Islam acknowledge the Five Pillars: they must profess the faith; pray five times a day facing the direction of the holy city of Mecca; give alms to the poor and to the mosque, which is the Muslim house of worship; fast during the month of Ramadan; and, if possible, visit Mecca in their lifetime.

Ancient Greece

By around 800 B.C., Greek farms and villages had expanded to form over 1,500 separate city-states in Greece and the surrounding area. Athens, the largest city-state, had a population of about 200,000 people by the year 500 B.C.

A great age of human achievement began as Greek civilization expanded. A love of beauty, a highly developed sense of civic duty, and a high value placed on ideas and discussion were the foundations of Greek society. The Greeks built public buildings and temples of glittering white marble, with brightly painted statues. Large crowds met for religious rites—including the first Olympic Games in 776 B.C., which then were part of a festival to honor the god Zeus.

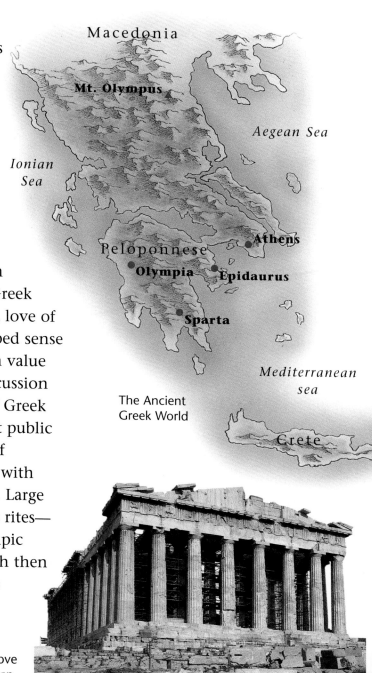

Macedonia

Mt. Olympus

Aegean Sea

Ionian Sea

Peloponnese

Olympia

Epidaurus

Athens

Sparta

Mediterranean sea

The Ancient Greek World

Crete

The Acropolis, built to honor the goddess Athena, stood above Athens, where it can still be seen.

With its powerful army and navy, Athens was the most important of the city-states. In the agora, the market plaza of Athens, Athenians met to discuss ideas and shop at the same time.

Athens produced great thinkers in the sixth century B.C. Men like Socrates, Aristotle, and Plato led discussions on what the world was like and how people should live. They were called philosophers (which means "lovers of wisdom"), and people still value their words today. Greeks examined the human body, observed the movements of stars and planets, and identified new animal species. Such work was the basis of modern medicine, astronomy, mathematics, and biology.

Greece's population grew so rapidly between 750 and 550 B.C. that the Greeks founded new colonies around the Mediterranean and Black seas, spreading their culture and expanding their influence.

Democracy

The word *democracy* comes from Greek words meaning "rule by the people." Although women, slaves, and those not born in Athens could not vote, Athenian democracy was direct: eligible citizens voted on how leaders should rule.

This vase shows Greeks discussing philosophy at a banquet.

The theater at Epidaurus seated 14,000 people.

The Greeks believed that their most important gods, led by the god Zeus, lived at the top of Mount Olympus. Poets recited or sang epics—long poems telling the adventures of gods and heroes. A few of these classic epics, especially the *Iliad* and *Odyssey* by the poet Homer, are still read today.

comic theater mask

By 500 B.C., staged dramas had become popular. Comedies and tragedies were performed at outdoor theaters before thousands of people. Archaeologists have found the ruins of ancient theaters all over Greece. Each actor played many roles, so masks were used to show changes in character or mood. Masks of tragedy and comedy are now symbols for the theater.

Sparta was a warlike city-state that ruled the south of Greece. Spartans and Athenians joined forces to defeat invading Persians in about 480 B.C., but within half a century the two cities had become rivals. They went to war in 431 B.C. By 404 B.C., Athens had been defeated and Sparta dominated the area for a short time. However, Sparta was soon defeated by the city-state of Thebes. This period began a decline of Greek power and influence.

ancient Greek soldier

It was a non-Greek, Alexander the Great, who spread Greek ideals across a huge empire. He was born in 356 B.C. in Macedonia, a country north of Greece. The Greek philosopher Aristotle was one of his teachers, and young Alexander grew up admiring Greece. Beginning when he was just twenty, Alexander led an army of Greeks and Macedonians to conquer Egypt, Judea, Persia, and part of India. He died of fever when he was only thirty-three, while he was planning an invasion of Arabia. His conquests spread Greek ideas throughout the eastern Mediterranean area.

Alexander the Great

The Roman Empire

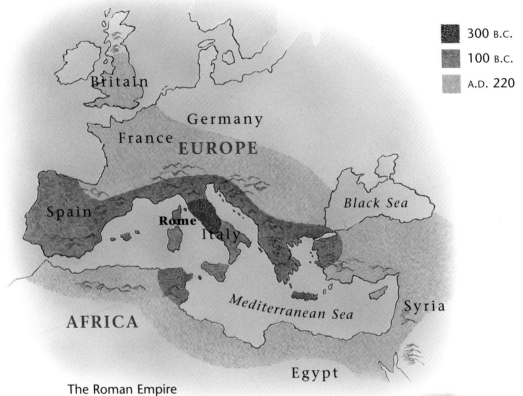

■	300 B.C.
■	100 B.C.
■	A.D. 220

The Roman Empire

The city of Rome was founded about 750 B.C. when several hill-farming villages joined together. At first ruled by kings, Rome formed a republic, an elected government, in about 500 B.C. Two leaders called consuls were elected each year to head the government. A lawmaking body called the senate passed laws. The Roman senate became a model for legislative bodies ever after.

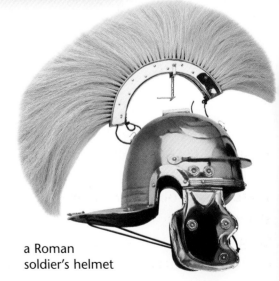

a Roman soldier's helmet

This Roman aqueduct runs through the town of Segovia in Spain.

The republic lasted for nearly 500 years. By 264 B.C., Rome had conquered all of what is now Italy. Around 49 B.C., however, civil wars broke out. Julius Caesar, a general, seized power but was killed by rivals in 44 B.C. After continued fighting, Caesar's nephew, Octavian, emerged as the victor. In 27 B.C. he took the title Augustus ("revered one") and became an absolute ruler, Rome's first emperor.

The empire grew to include most of Europe, North Africa, and part of the Middle East. At its heart was Rome, which by A.D. 300 had a population of 1 million. Wealthy Romans lived in houses with painted walls and beautifully tiled floors. The poor of Rome lived in overcrowded, badly built apartments that often collapsed.

Long, straight roads helped speed armies, goods, and messages throughout the empire. Channels constructed of stone, called aqueducts, brought water from the countryside. Only wealthy homes had running water, but there were public drinking fountains, restrooms, and hot and cold public baths.

The emperors created popular spectacles at Rome's Colosseum. Bears, tigers, lions, and elephants fought against each other and against men. Slaves and criminals were trained as gladiators, or fighters. People cheered for their favorites. Archaeologists found one gladiator's name scrawled on a wall with the phrase "the man the girls sigh for."

The Roman family was centered around the father, who had total power. Parents arranged children's marriages. Usually women ran households, but some women were chosen to become priestesses, and a very few had businesses or professions. Boys from wealthy Roman families went to school or studied with private tutors, starting at age six. Boys studied reading, writing, and mathematics at first; later, history, literature, and astronomy were added. Girls were usually taught household skills, and poor children were given no education at all.

ivory hair comb

This picture is from the tomb of a wealthy Roman woman. Note her hair style, jewelry, and elegant dress.

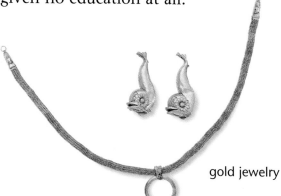

gold jewelry

The Romans worshiped gods similar to those of Greece, but belief in them faded over time. Christianity, forbidden at first by the Emperor Nero, grew throughout the empire. Then Emperor Constantine, who ruled Rome from A.D. 306 to 337, became a Christian and ended the persecution of Christians. The faith was legalized with the Edict of Milan in 313.

This gold coin shows Constantine, the first Christian Roman emperor.

The greatest period of the Roman Empire lasted until about A.D. 200. Gradually, however, the empire came under attack from Germanic tribes to the north and Persians in the east. In 395 rivalries split the great empire into two parts. The eastern capital was Constantinople, founded by Constantine in 330. Greek-speaking emperors, the Byzantines, ruled the eastern land for another thousand years. The western part fell in 476 to attacking Visigoths, a fierce tribe from what is now Germany.

The Roman influence on modern civilization lives on almost everywhere. Romans founded cities such as London (Londinium), and their ideas about government and law are still part of societies today. Roman ideas in art, science, religion, and language have influenced generations the world over.

Skilled Craftspeople

A skilled Roman craftsperson made this cosmetics flask by blowing a bubble of hot liquid glass into a mold. Molds allowed for mass production of many useful everyday items.

The Celts of Europe

The Celts (pronounced KELTS) first appeared in what is now Austria about 700 B.C. They were skilled horseback riders and metalworkers. Over the next 500 years they spread to Gaul (France), Spain, England, Ireland, Scotland and Wales, and other parts of Europe.

The Celts belonged to tribes led by an aristocracy, or noble class, of chiefs, warriors, priests, and poets. Most Celts were farmers who lived in villages in round, thatched houses. They kept cattle, pigs, and sheep, and made flour from wheat and barley. Craftspeople spun and wove sheep's wool into cloth. They also built hilltop forts and islands in lakes for defense.

Scotland

Scandinavia

North Sea

Ireland

Wales

England

Germany

ATLANTIC OCEAN

France

Austria

Spain

Italy

Mediterranean Sea

The Celtic World

bronze mirror with typical swirling Celtic pattern, c. 50 B.C.– A.D. 50

This is what a Celtic village in Wales may have looked like.

The Celts' skill at metalwork enabled them to make strong chariots, armor, and iron weapons, which helped them in battle. Archaeologists also have found many beautiful Celtic objects of bronze, iron, copper, and gold. Aristocrats' belongings were often decorated with complex patterns.

The Celts passed on their history and legends through storytelling and poetry. They honored their heroes with songs learned by heart and sung to harp music. One famous legend that came from Celtic tales is that of King Arthur. His court may actually have existed in the sixth century A.D. Stories describing the courageous Knights of the Round Table had their beginnings in the values of the Celtic warrior-culture in ancient Britain. The legends of Arthur have survived for more than a thousand years.

In the legends of King Arthur, a Round Table was inscribed with the knights' names. This replica table hangs in Winchester Castle, England.

Africa

Many scientists believe that human beings originated in the Rift Valley in Africa millions of years ago. Until about 3,000 years ago, people south of the Sahara desert lived in small family groups, hunting game and gathering plant foods. Beginning about 1000 B.C., they learned to farm and raise livestock. Bantu-speaking people of the western forests learned to make iron tools and weapons. Using these tools, they spread south and east. About 500 B.C. they settled the Congo River area. By A.D. 400 they had expanded their territory to include southern Africa.

Mediterranean Sea

Arabia

Egypt

Sahara Desert

Nubia

Kush

Red Sea

AFRICA

Meroë

Axum

Ghana

Benin

Gold Coast

Congo

Rift Valley

Shona

Great Zimbabwe

African Kingdoms

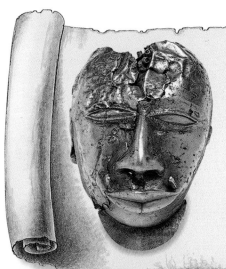

Ashanti Gold

Gold was plentiful in western Africa. It was important for trade. It also inspired local goldsmiths to make sculptures and ornaments. The Ashanti people of Ghana have one of the best-known traditions. Ashanti craftspeople made this golden head to honor a chief killed in battle.

Because they were isolated by the great Sahara desert, these rich and complex societies had only occasional contact with others from the north and east. However, merchants from the Mediterranean sailed around the coast of Africa to trade for gold, sandalwood, and kola nuts.

In eastern Africa, trading kingdoms such as Meroë (590 B.C.–A.D. 300) and Axum (c. A.D. 50–650) arose. The Kush and Nubian people, who ruled Egypt for a time around 700 B.C., gradually moved southward and founded Meroë in the third century B.C. People of this civilization developed an alphabet, cultivated cotton, and used waterwheels for irrigation.

Ivory, incense, spices, and other valuable goods were shipped from Red Sea ports to Mediterranean lands and India. Great Zimbabwe, the capital of the Shona empire in southern Africa, was a granite-walled city of about 10,000 people, until it was mysteriously abandoned in A.D. 1450. The forest kingdom of Benin, in what is now Nigeria, traded with Portugal. These societies show how people around the world developed civilization in similar ways.

the walled city of
Great Zimbabwe

China

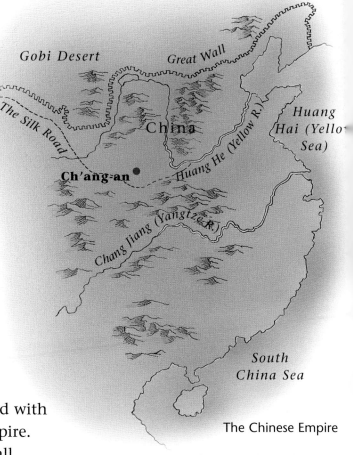

The Chinese Empire

A brilliant, ruthless general named Zheng united China in 221 B.C. by conquering many separate warring states. His own state was called Ch'in (now called Qin), and his empire is now called China after it. Zheng built roads to link his lands, established a written language, and established uniform laws, weights, and measures. Although he destroyed books he did not like, and killed scholars who disagreed with him, he made China an empire.

Zheng ordered a great wall to be built to protect China from attacks by northern tribes. Although it took many centuries to complete the Great Wall of China, it was begun during Zheng's reign. Many workers died while building it, and they were buried where they fell. When Zheng died in 210 B.C., he was buried with an army of 7,500 life-size terra cotta (pottery) soldiers to protect him.

Zheng's life-size pottery army was buried with him.

the Great Wall
of China today

China Ware

We call cups and plates "china" after the fine porcelain created in China during the Tang dynasty. Along with tea, silk, and other precious goods, Chinese porcelain traveled to Europe along the Silk Road, a trade route.

The Tang dynasty came to power in A.D. 618, bringing an era of peace to China. The Tang capital, Ch'ang-an, which means "Forever Safe," was the largest city in the world at the time, with more than a million residents. The wealthy wore silk clothes and enjoyed music, poetry, painting, and games such as chess and cards. Tang emperors cut back the power of nobles, distributed land more fairly, and developed trade with neighboring countries.

The Tang emperors valued the arts and music, and poetry was especially important. Artisans from these dynasties crafted beautiful paintings and pottery, many of which have survived to this day.

A trade route called the "Silk Road" stretched from China to the Middle East, covering more than 4,350 miles. Chinese merchants traveled along it with silk, tea, salt, paper, and porcelain, and brought back horses, furs, spices, and gold. This route also began to connect the distant civilizations of the countries it traveled through.

This wheelbarrow is one of many Chinese inventions. The Chinese also invented printing, and in A.D. 868 they printed the world's first book.

Aboriginal Australian Peoples

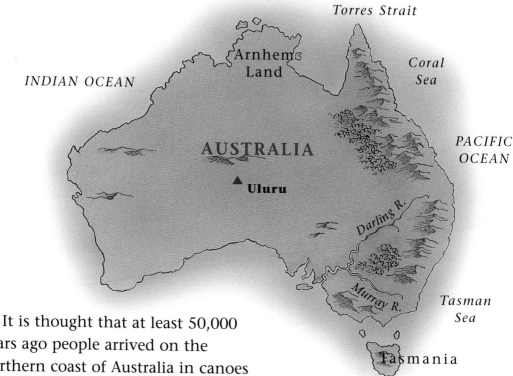

Torres Strait

Arnhem Land

INDIAN OCEAN

Coral Sea

AUSTRALIA

PACIFIC OCEAN

▲ Uluru

Darling R.

Murray R.

Tasman Sea

Tasmania

It is thought that at least 50,000 years ago people arrived on the northern coast of Australia in canoes or on rafts. They had sailed from Southeast Asia, which in those days was only 40 miles away because sea levels were lower. As a result, land areas along the coast were larger than they are today. At first the people settled near the coasts, but gradually they moved across the continent. They inhabited different kinds of land, including rain forests, mountains, and deserts.

Aboriginal Australians perform a ceremonial dance.

These people were the ancestors of today's Aboriginal Australians. The desert people were nomads, moving in small groups in search of food. In forested areas, people settled for months at a time. In Arnhem Land in the north of the continent, they built huts on raised wooden platforms to protect against seasonal flooding. Tamed wild dogs called dingoes guarded the shelters and provided warmth on cold nights.

The Aboriginal people's connection to the land, and to its animals and plants, is essential to Aboriginal culture, as are art and religion. Aboriginal petroglyphs, or rock carvings, may date back more than 30,000 years.

Dingoes were used as guard dogs.

Modern Aboriginal Australians carry on many of their ancestors' beliefs and customs. They believe that the world was created during Dreamtime, or *Tjukurrpa*. During Dreamtime ancestral beings (including the sun, wind, rain, animals, plants, and humans) roamed Earth. It was the duty of humans to look after the land.

People draw pictures and tell stories about the Dreamtime and hold ceremonial dances that re-enact the past. Uluru, also known as Ayers Rock, is a huge sandstone monolith in central Australia. It is a sacred site and has pictures that illustrate Dreamtime stories painted or carved on it.

This returning boomerang was used for driving small flocks of birds into nets. With a heavier, non-returning boomerang, a person could bring down game or an enemy up to 500 feet away.

Uluru is a sacred Aboriginal site.

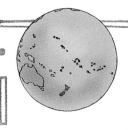

Polynesia and New Zealand

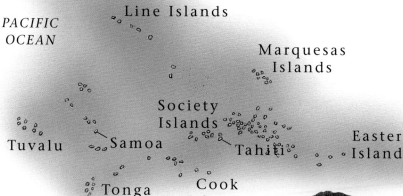

Hawaiian Islands

Polynesian islands dot the vast Pacific Ocean.

Line Islands

PACIFIC OCEAN

Marquesas Islands

Society Islands

New Zealand

Tuvalu   Samoa

Tahiti

Easter Island

Tonga   Cook Islands

Four thousand years ago, people sailed from the islands of Southeast Asia to make new homes on the Polynesian islands of the Pacific Ocean. First, they settled Tonga and Samoa. By A.D. 100, they had reached Hawaii, and by A.D. 400, Easter Island, where they built huge, mysterious stone statues of faces.

Polynesian sailors navigated not only by the sun and stars but also by wind, wave, and cloud patterns, and by observing the behavior of land-based birds. Their dugout canoes, with matted palm-leaf sails, could carry people as well as food, animals, and seeds.

Some of the mysterious statues on Easter Island weigh as much as 50 tons, yet no one knows how they were moved from the quarry where they were carved to their current location by the sea.

Each island community formed its own way of life, but most had chiefs. Polynesians fished, grew sweet potatoes, yams, taro, bananas, and breadfruit, and raised animals. They used the coconut palm for food, timber, house thatching, and basket material.

About A.D. 950, the Polynesians reached an uninhabited island they called Aotearoa. Later, Europeans named it New Zealand. New Zealand was one of the last places on Earth to be inhabited.

The Maori, as these first inhabitants were called, arrived from a legendary land they called Hawaiki, which for a long time was thought to be Tahiti. New archaeological evidence suggests that this is probably untrue, that they came from Taiwan or Melanesia or perhaps both.

This Maori battle axe is made of basalt rock.

Maori villages were usually guarded by a fort. The people were divided into tribes, or *iwi*, each made up of descendants of a common ancestor. Each tribe was made up of a number of *hapu*, or clans, which in turn were composed of family groups called *whanau*. Primogeniture, or inheritance by the firstborn son, was basic to the social system and determined the succession of the highest chief.

This system remained in place until Europeans arrived in the 1600s. At first the Maori welcomed Europeans, but as their culture became increasingly disrupted they resisted. Although ancient Maori society has nearly disappeared, it remains today in language, song, and respect for the land and sea.

Polynesian boat

Native American Civilizations

Many scientists believe that the first settlers walked into North America from Asia about 20,000 years ago. They migrated during the last ice age, when the two continents were joined by a land bridge. By A.D. 1500, there were perhaps 1.3 million Native Americans, making up more than 300 different cultures. There were Inuit hunters in the Arctic north, farmers in the forested east, and fishing and whaling groups in the coastal northwest.

Nomadic tribes hunted buffalo on the grassy plains between the Rocky Mountains and the Mississippi River and horticulturists lived in the Southeast. The Hohokam and the Anasazi lived in the southwestern desert from about the first to the fourteenth century A.D. Late in that period they built cliffside apartment villages of adobe (dried mud) bricks and dug canals to irrigate their crops.

Arctic

Northwest Coast

Subarctic

Plateau

Northeast

Great Basin

Great Plains

California

Southwest

Southeast

Native American cultures were shaped by the geography, climate, and resources of ten different regions.

Great Plains teepee

Native American cultures changed over time. People learned from each other as they fought or became allies. Farming and building methods and artistic styles changed. Drought or war caused migrations.

The most dramatic changes were brought about by contact with Europeans. The Spanish brought horses to the New World in the 1500s. Over time, Native American groups began to acquire horses. Plains tribes no longer had to hunt buffalo or fight wars on foot. Europeans pushed native peoples off their lands and brought diseases, such as measles and smallpox, which killed thousands of people. By the 1900s, Native American populations were declining, and a way of life nearly ended.

Native Americans were the first to cultivate about 75 percent of the many varieties of food grown in the world today. Many medicines in current use were first discovered by Native American healers centuries before the Europeans came to North America. If not for the help generously offered by Native Americans to early explorers and expeditions, early European settlements might never have survived.

war headdress of the Cheyenne Chief White Eagle

Carved Poles

Totem poles of the Northwest tribes told stories. They could also be a carved picture record of the "family tree." Many are 40 feet tall.

The Incas

The Inca people forged South America's biggest empire. Once a small farming tribe, they defeated neighboring peoples and built cities such as Cuzco, their capital. In valleys they grew maize (corn); in the highlands they grew potatoes on irrigated terraces. Inca women wove beautiful textiles of alpaca and llama wool. The Incas were also known for making many fine objects of gold, silver, and turquoise.

The Incas built paved roads throughout their empire. Relay runners covered 150 miles per day and carried coded messages of knotted string called *quipus*. In their search for gold, Spanish conquerors, led by Francisco Pizarro, destroyed the empire in 1532.

Andes Mountains

Inca Road

Machu Picchu

Cuzco

PACIFIC OCEAN

Inca Road

The Inca Empire

Mountain City

These are the ruins of Machu Picchu, an Inca city high in the Andes. Machu Picchu was ignored and later forgotten by Spanish colonial authorities. Hiram Bingham, an American explorer, rediscovered the site in 1911.

The Past and the Future

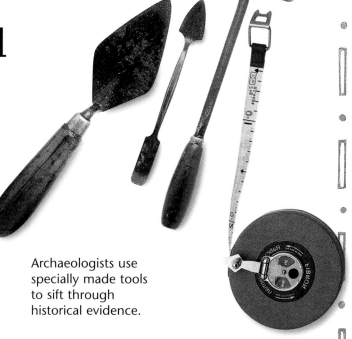

In this book you have seen how many civilizations around the world found ways to organize, provide food, make objects they needed or wanted, build cities, defend themselves, and learn about the world around them.

Archaeologists use specially made tools to sift through historical evidence.

Sometimes the efforts of ancient peoples were similar, even though they were separated by time and distance. Ancient peoples around the Mediterranean and in the South Pacific, for example, both studied navigation.

The work of learning about the past continues. Each year new discoveries are made about the lives and ways of ancient peoples that help us better understand how our world came to be as it is. Perhaps in the future scholars will study how we lived in order to understand their own world better.

Excavations, such as this one at Jericho in the eastern Mediterranean region, help us to learn about the past.

Index